Sea Life

Coloring Book for Adults

Max Fleming

ISBN: 9798688141344

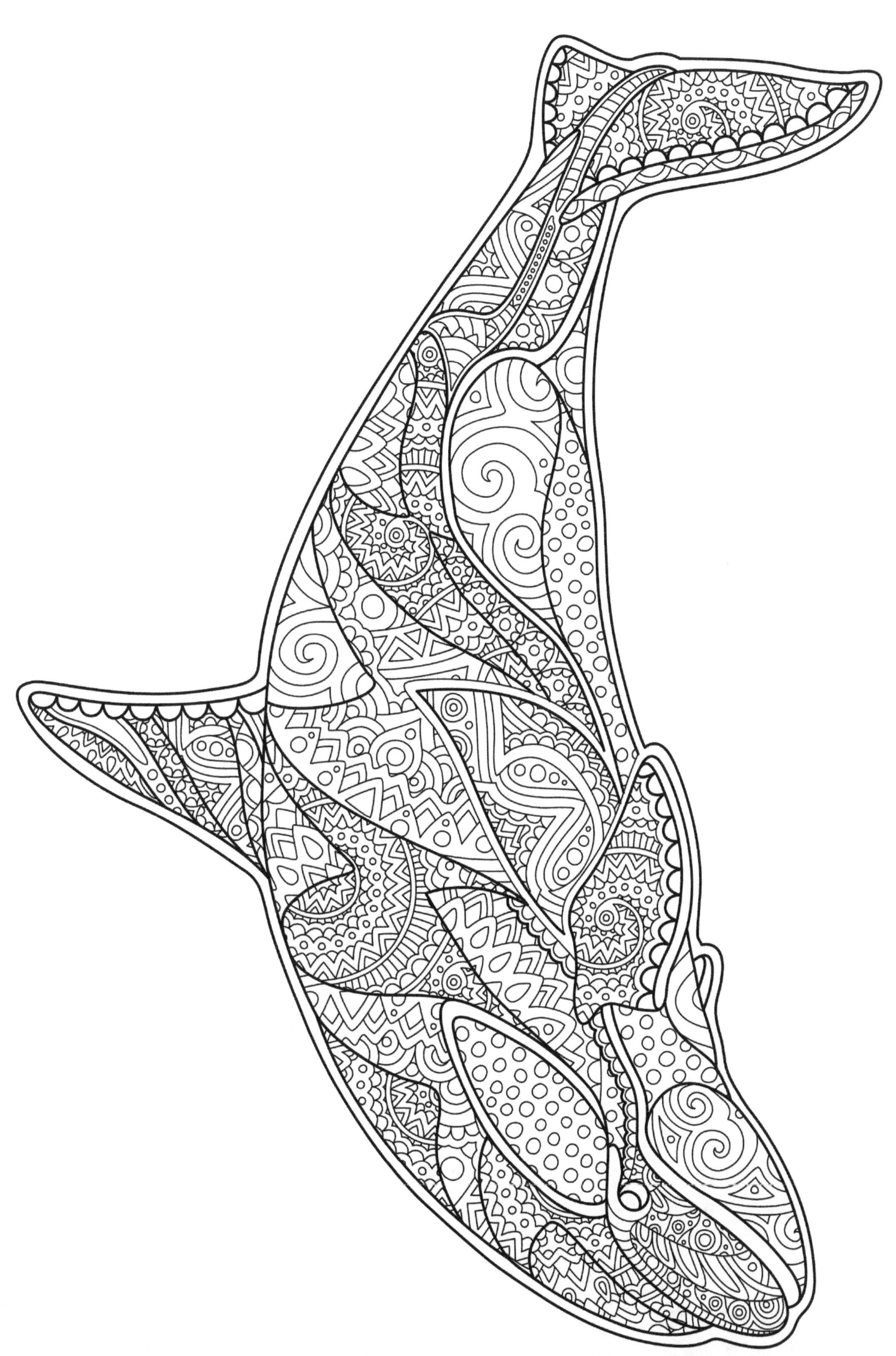

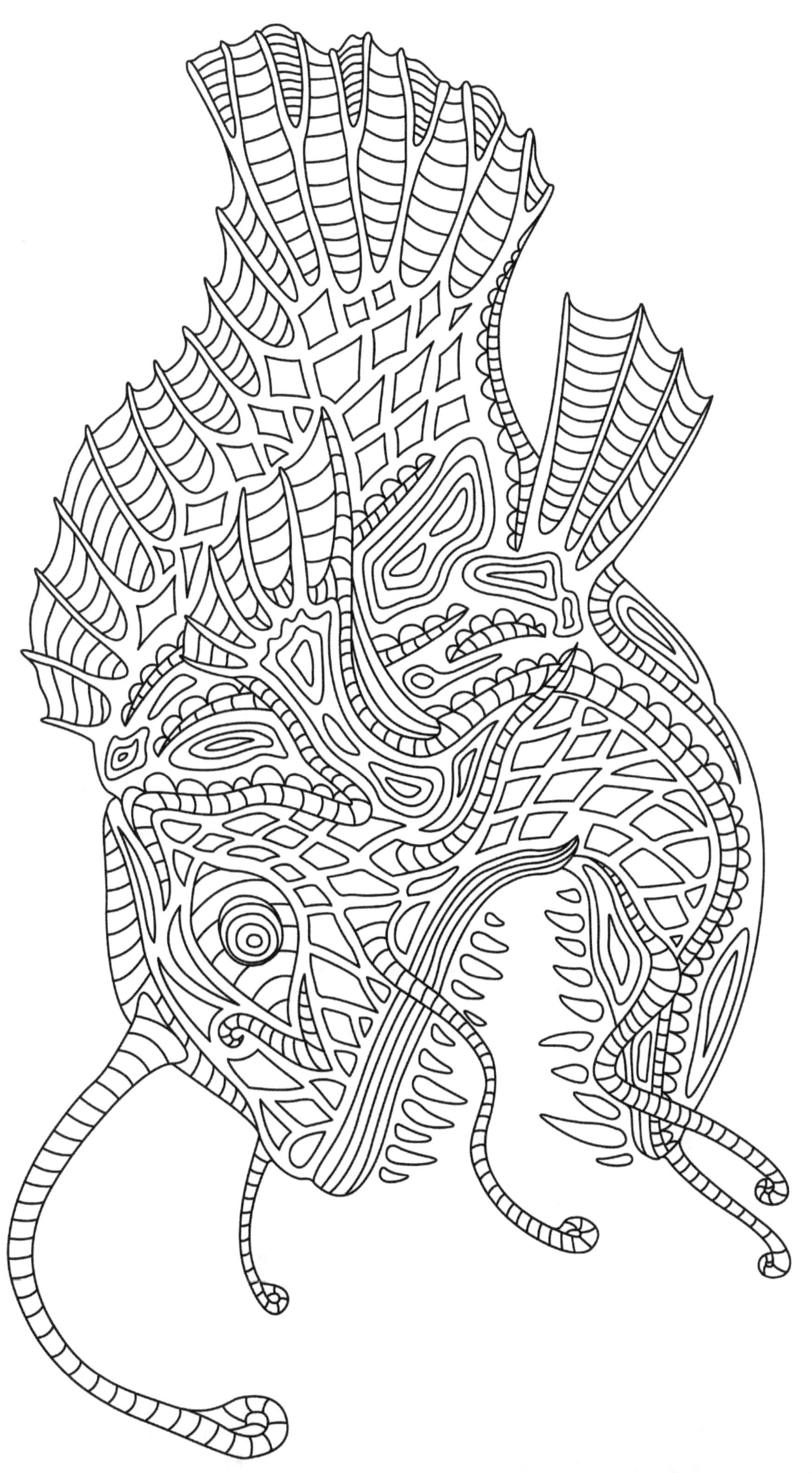

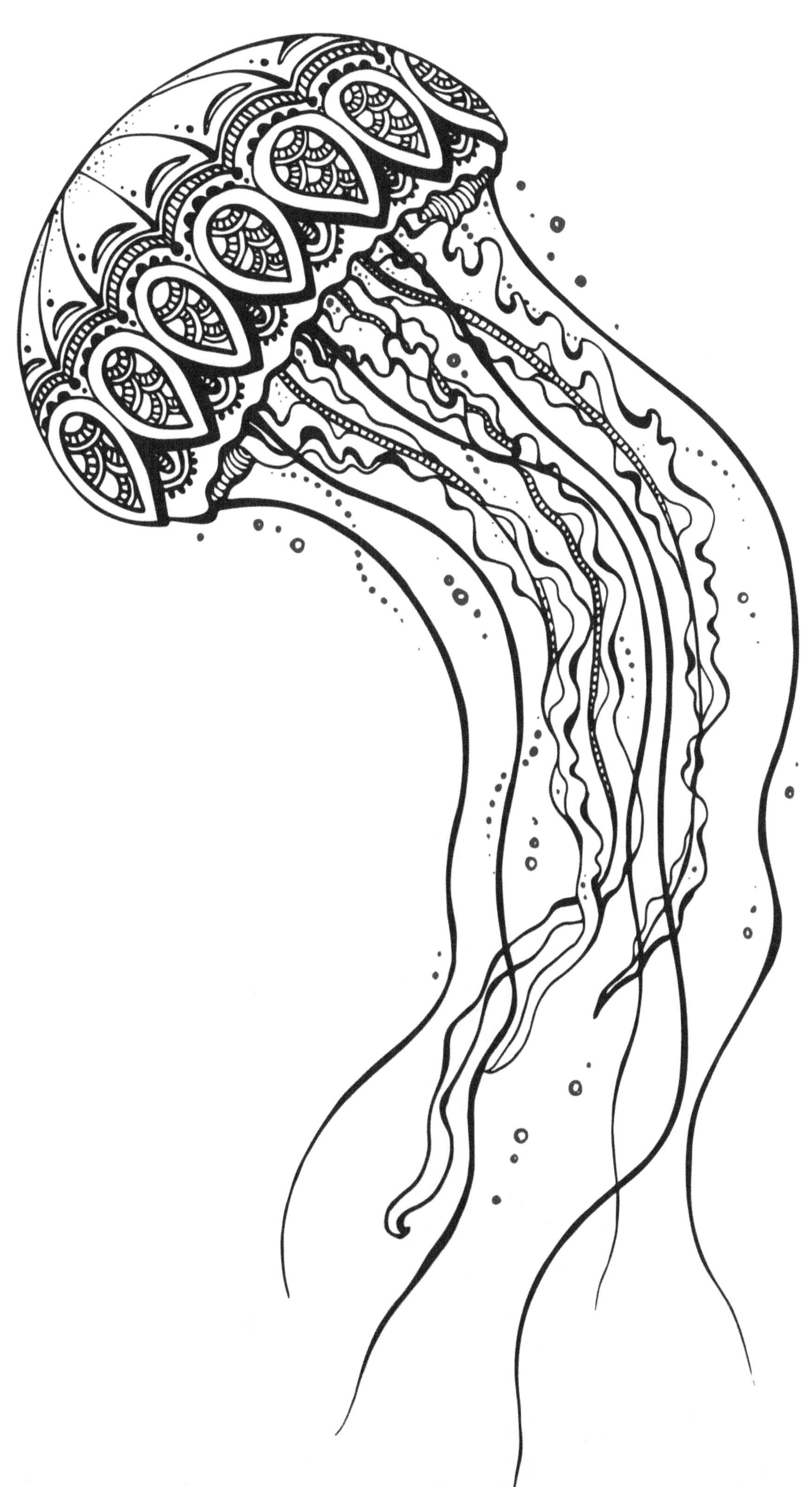

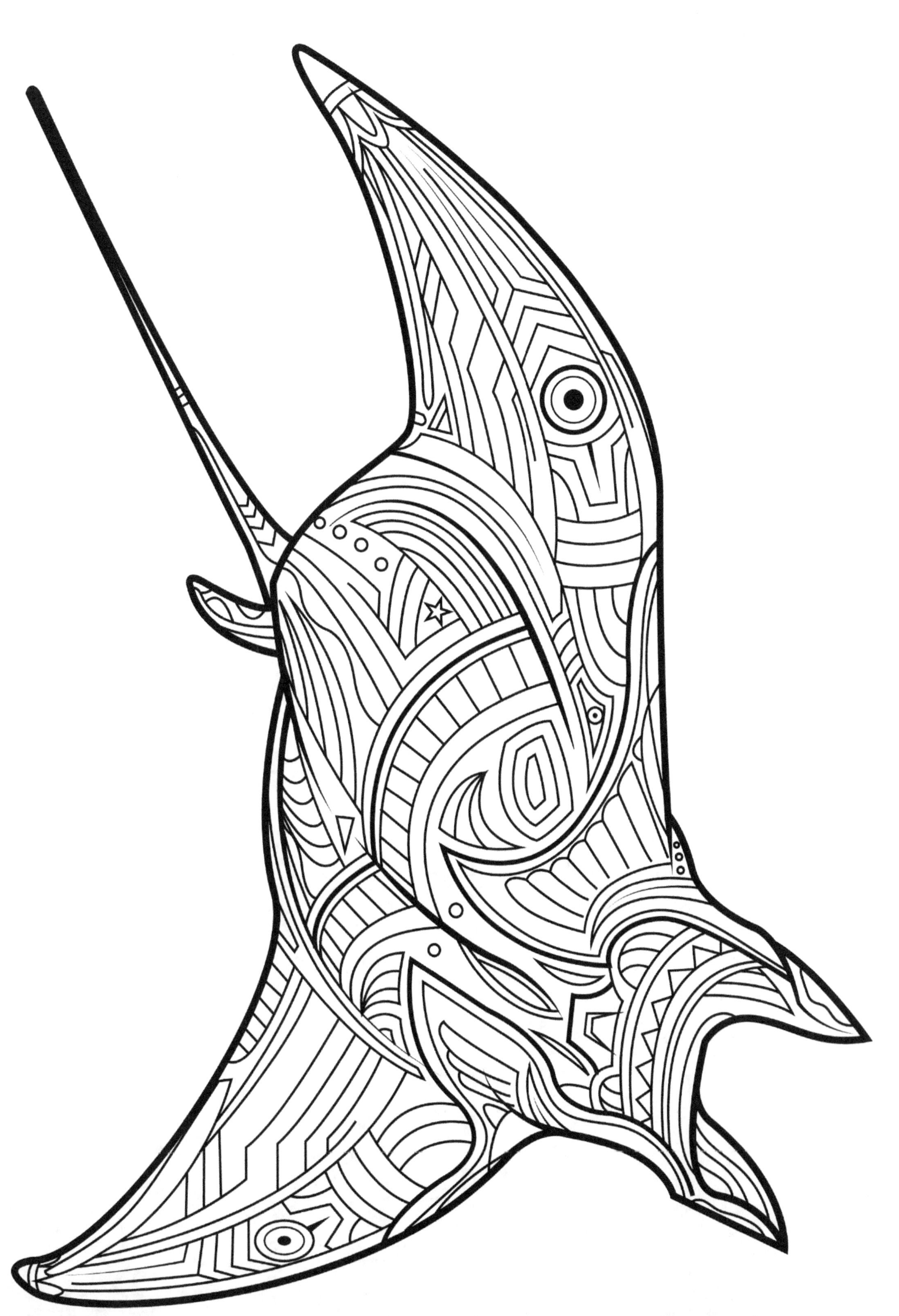

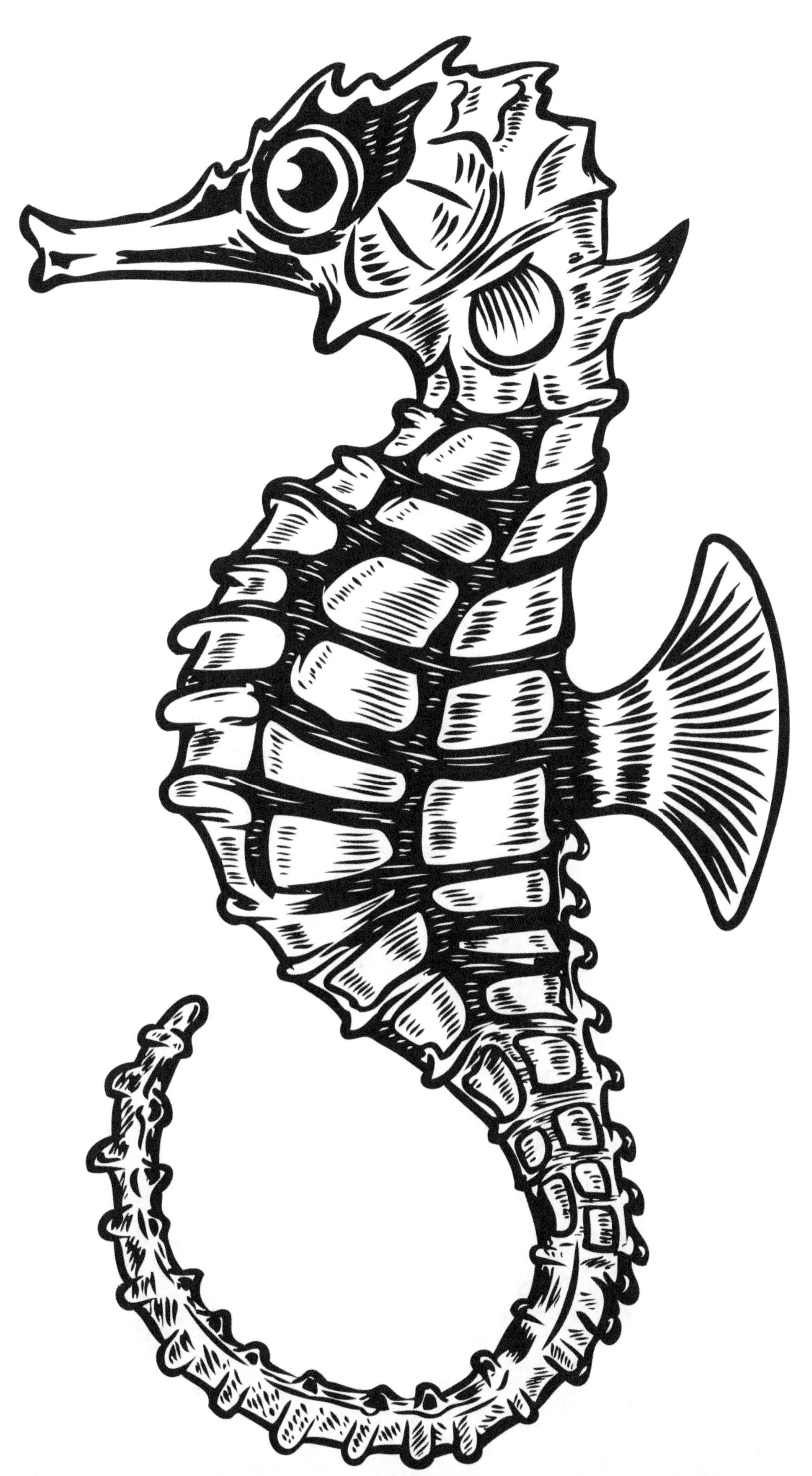

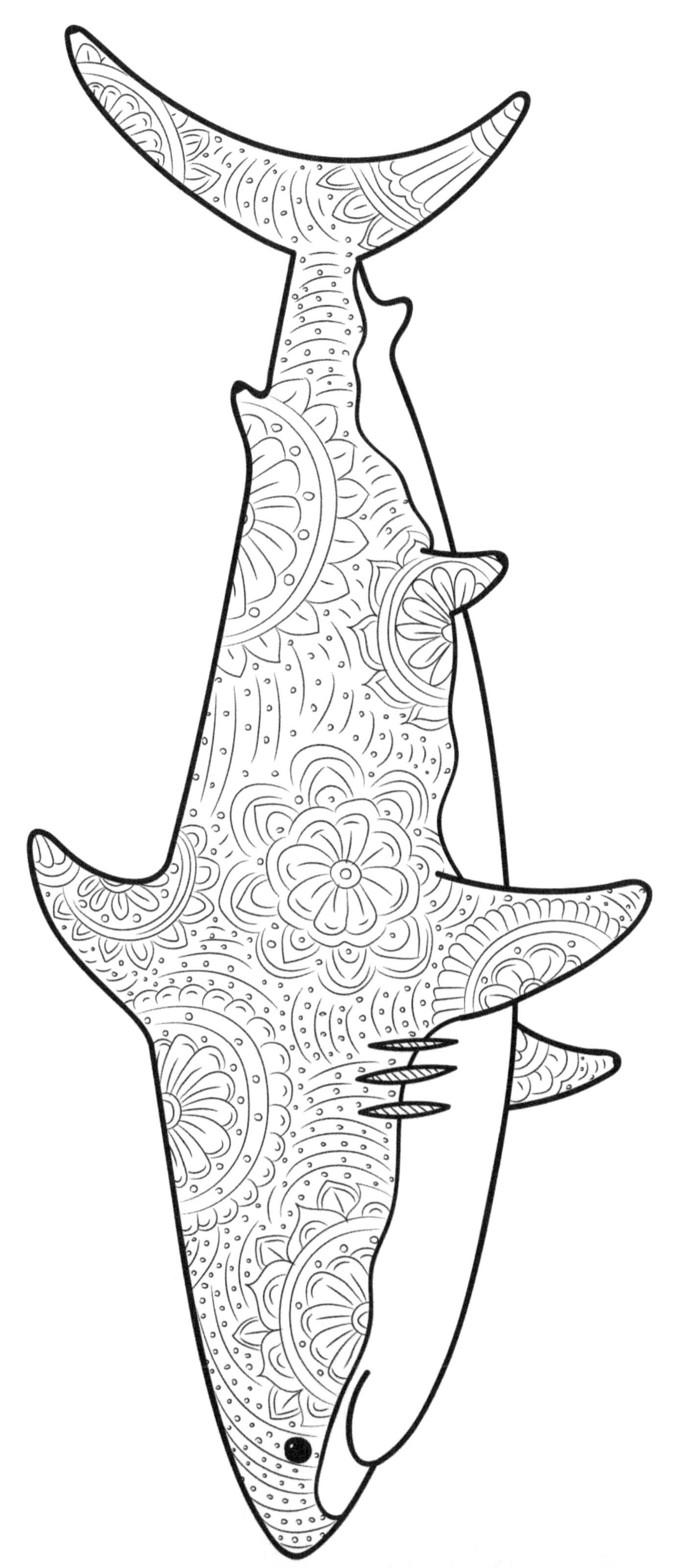

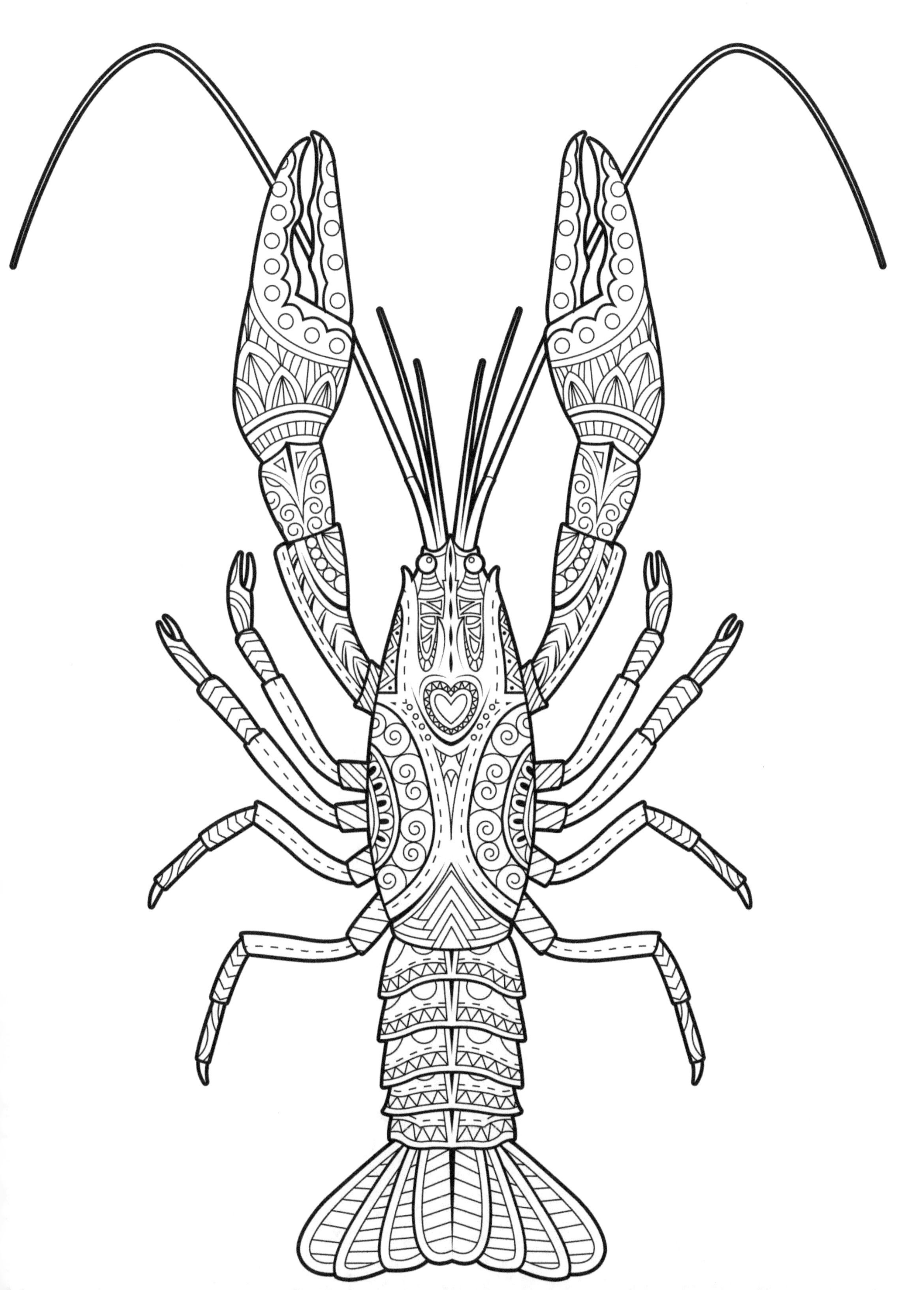

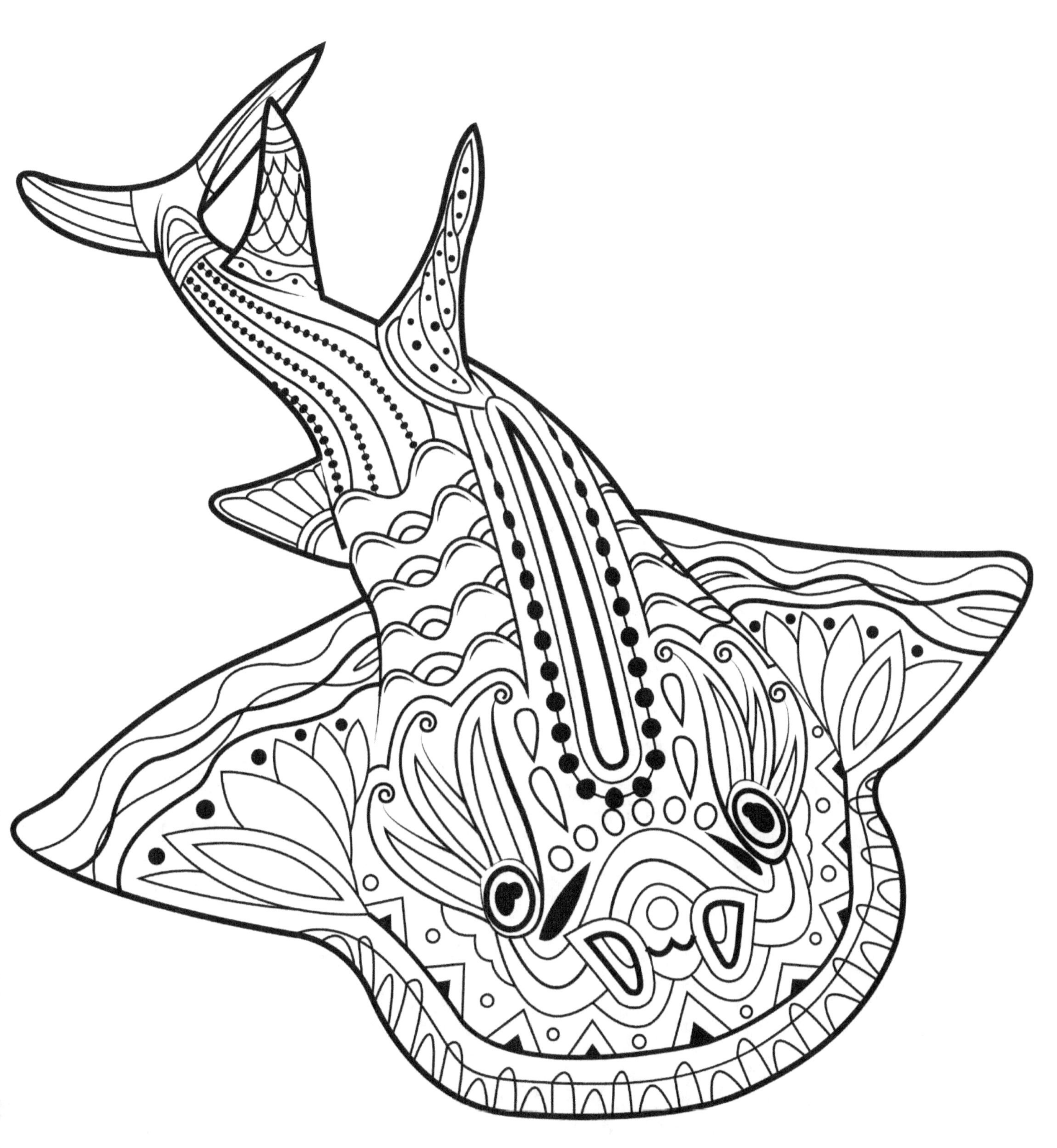